Disney
Tangled
MUSIC FROM THE MOTION PICTURE SOUNDTRACK

Disney characters and artwork © Disney Enterprises, Inc.

ISBN 978-1-4584-0844-0

WALT DISNEY MUSIC COMPANY
WONDERLAND MUSIC COMPANY, INC.

DISTRIBUTED BY

HAL•LEONARD® CORPORATION

7777 W. BLUEMOUND RD. P.O. BOX 13819 MILWAUKEE, WI 53213

In Australia Contact:
Hal Leonard Australia Pty. Ltd.
4 Lentara Court
Cheltenham, Victoria, 3192 Australia
Email: ausadmin@halleonard.com.au

Visit Hal Leonard Online at
www.halleonard.com

WHEN WILL MY LIFE BEGIN

Music by ALAN MENKEN
Lyrics by GLENN SLATER

Moderately fast Rock

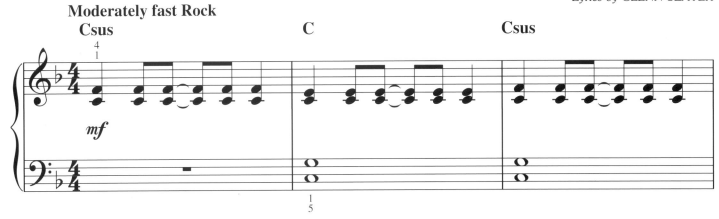

Rapunzel: Sev-en a. m.,___ the u - su - al morn-ing
Then af - ter lunch,_ it's puz - zles, and darts and

line - up._____ Start on the chores,__ and sweep_ 'til the floor's all
bak - ing..._____ pa - per mâ - ché,__ a bit___ of bal - let and

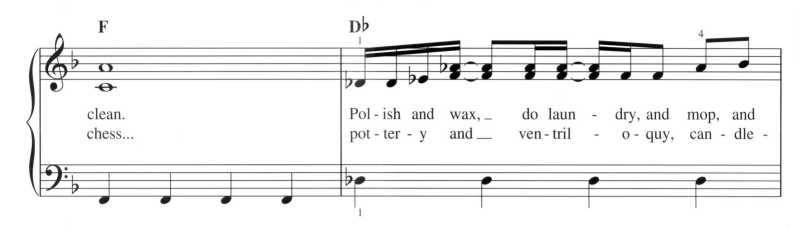

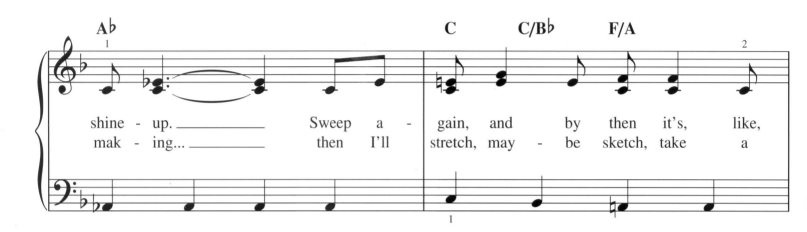

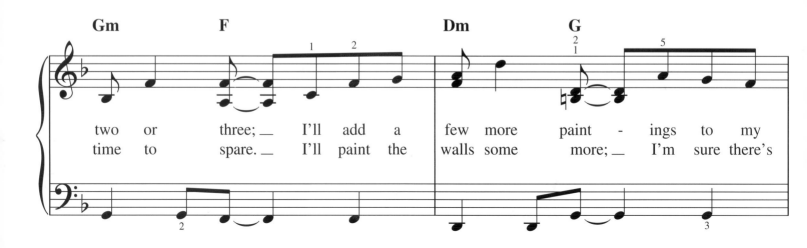

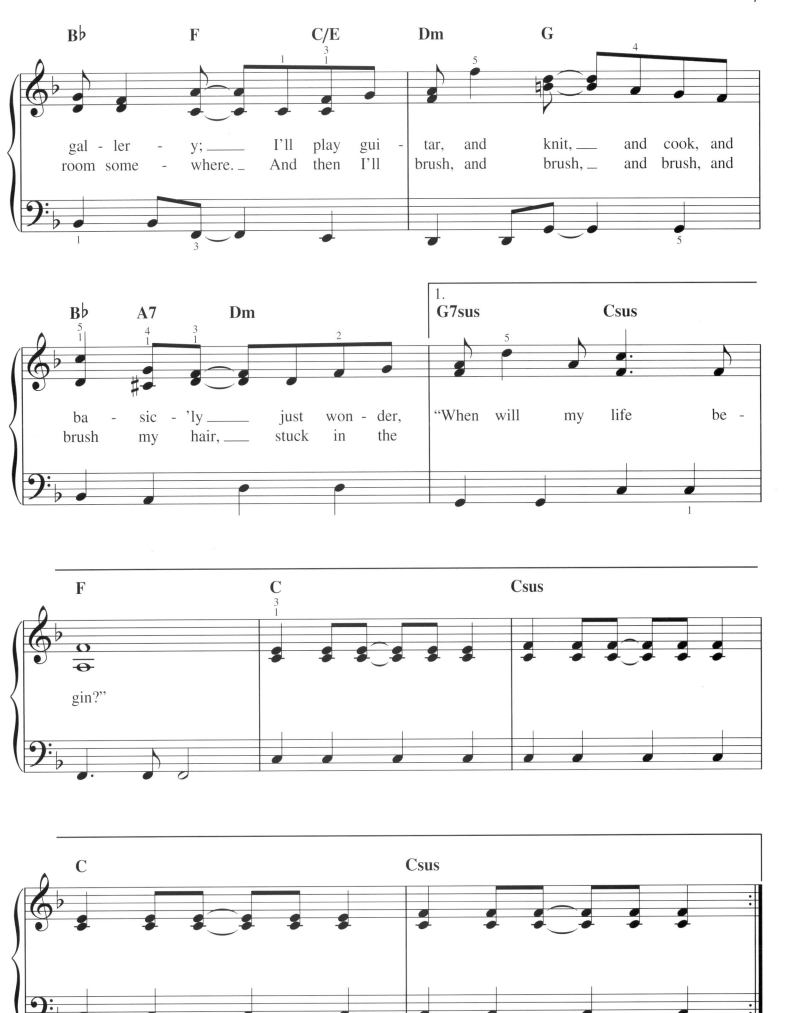

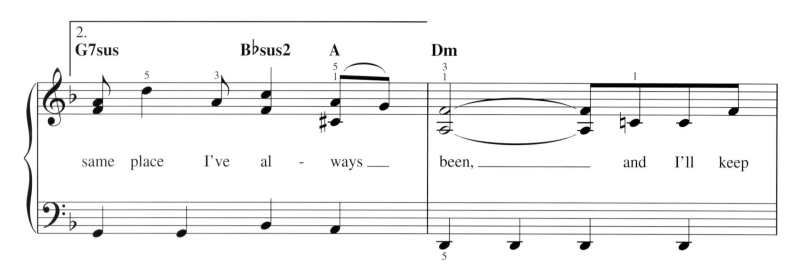

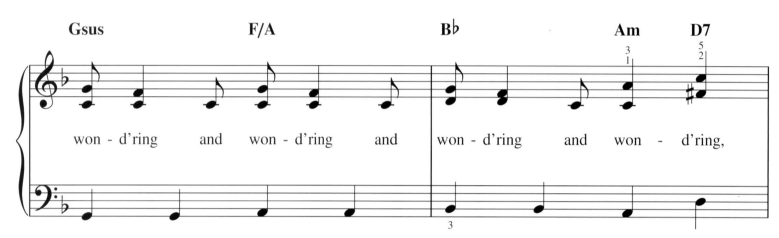

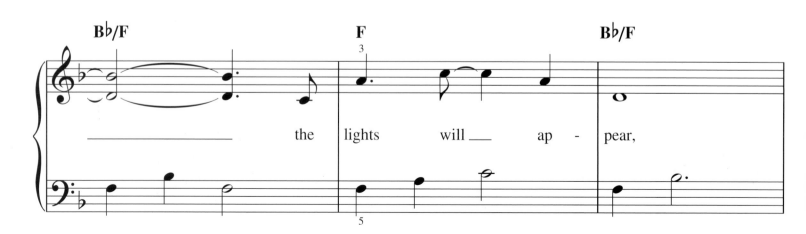

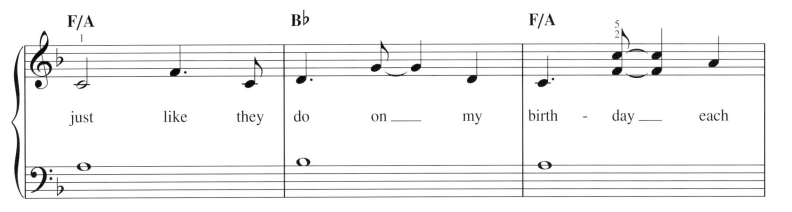

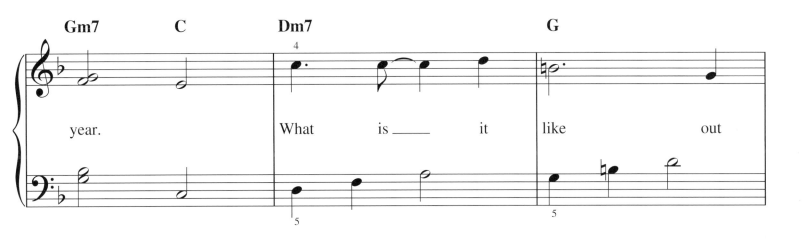

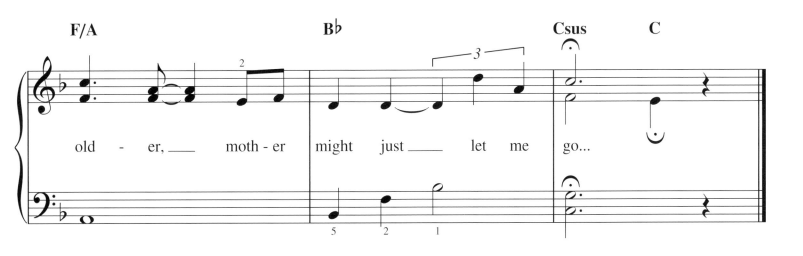

MOTHER KNOWS BEST

Music by ALAN MENKEN
Lyrics by GLENN SLATER

Moderately, with rubato

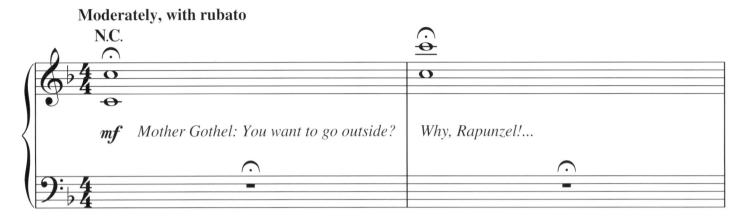

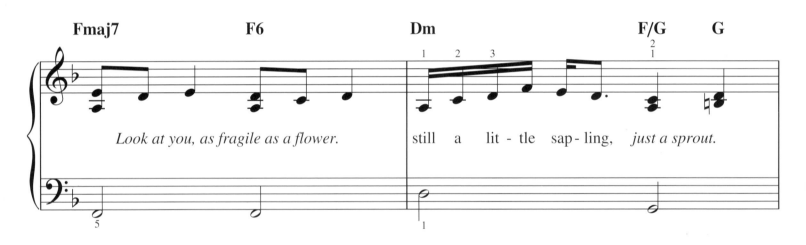

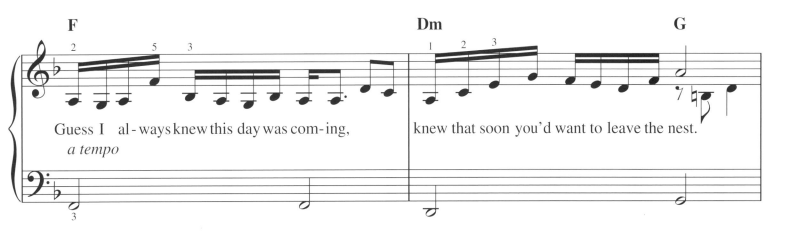

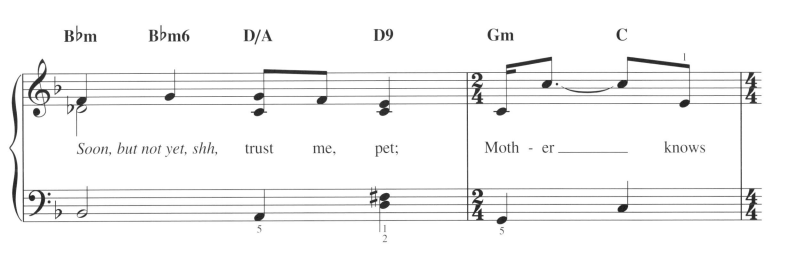

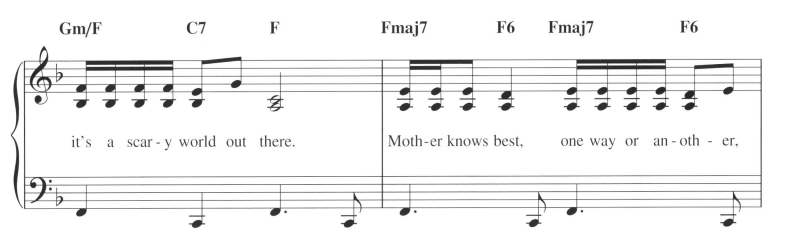

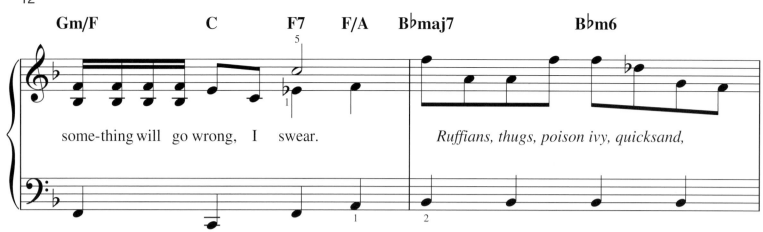

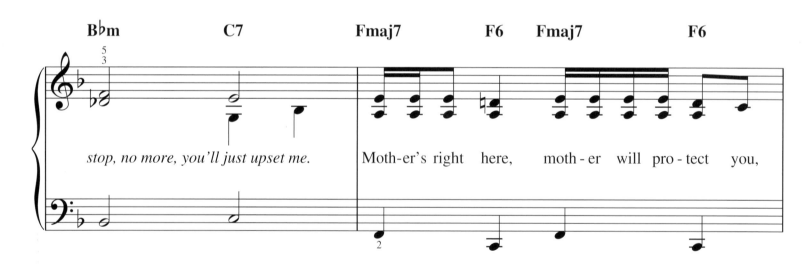

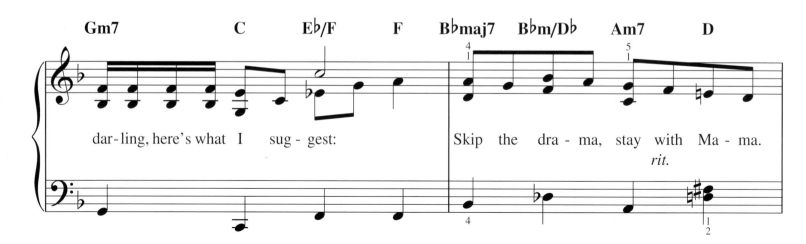

A tempo

Rapunzel: Yes, Mother.

Mother Gothel: I love you very much, dear.

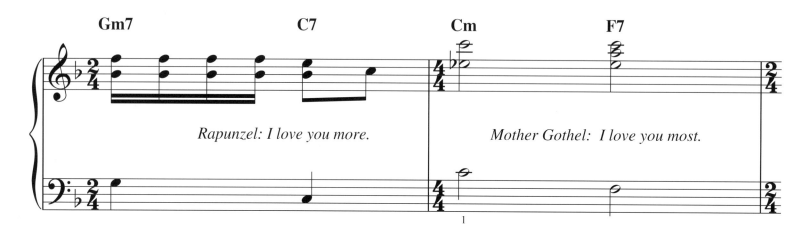

Rapunzel: I love you more.

Mother Gothel: I love you most.

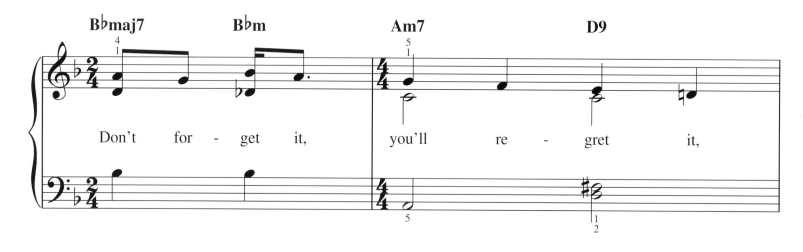

Don't for - get it, you'll re - gret it,

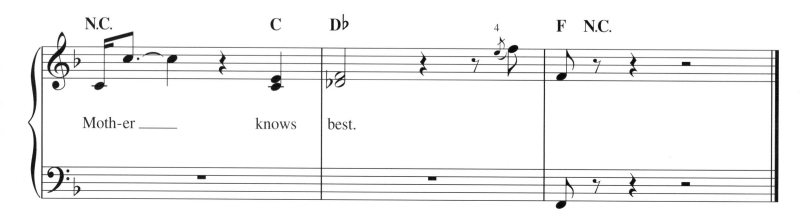

Moth-er _____ knows best.

I'VE GOT A DREAM

Music by ALAN MENKEN
Lyrics by GLENN SLATER

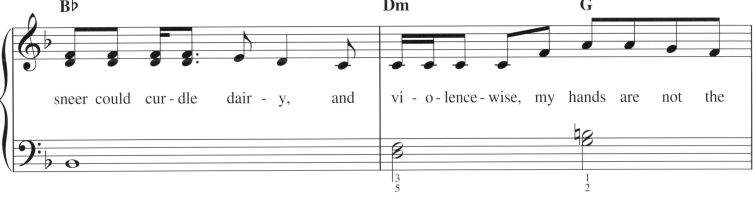

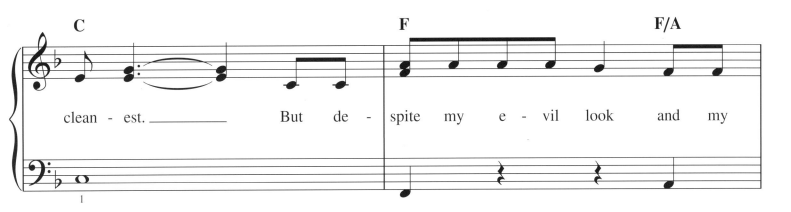

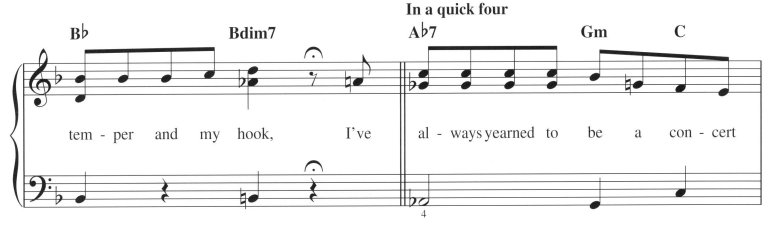

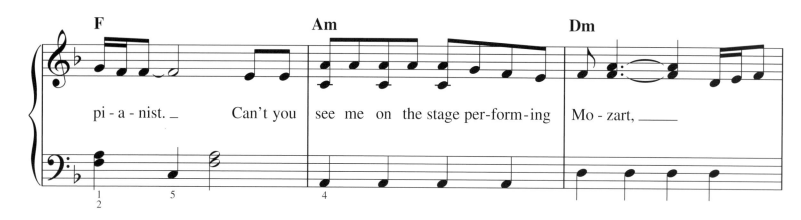

pi - a - nist. _ Can't you see me on the stage per-form-ing Mo - zart, _____

tick-l-ing the i-v'ries 'til they gleam? Yep, I'd rath-er be called dead-ly for my

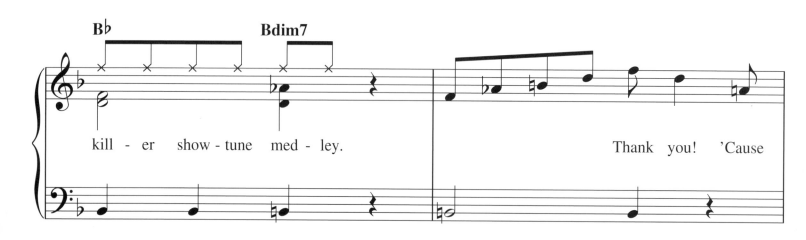

kill - er show - tune med - ley. Thank you! 'Cause

way down deep in-side, I've got a dream. _____ He's got a dream, _____ he's got a

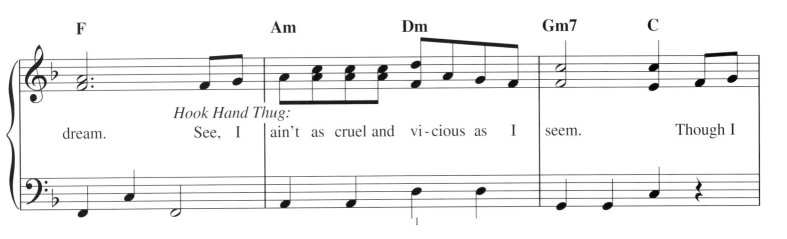

dream.   *Hook Hand Thug:* See, I ain't as cruel and vi-cious as I   seem.   Though I

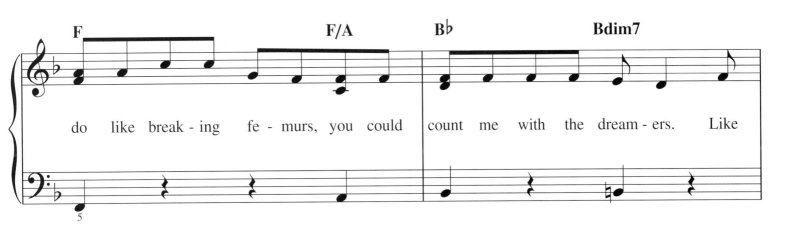

do   like break-ing fe - murs, you could   count me with the dream - ers.   Like

ev - 'ry - bod - y else, I've got a   dream.   *Thug Chorus:* Na na   na   na   na   na   na   na   na

na   na   na   na   na. *Big Nose Thug:* I've got   scars and lumps and bruis - es, ___ plus

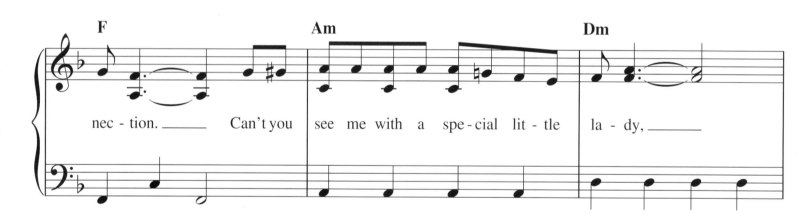

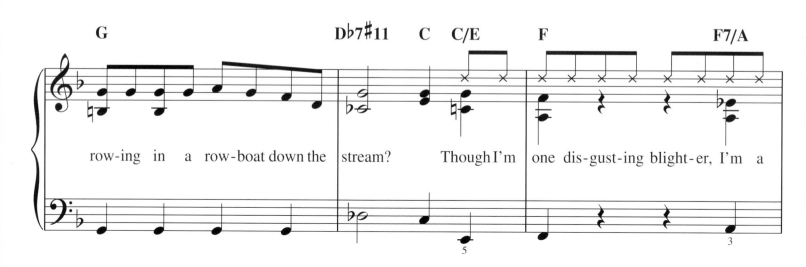

lov-er, not a fight-er, 'cause way down deep in-side, I've got a dream. I've got a

dream, _____ I've got a dream, and I know one day ro-mance will reign su-

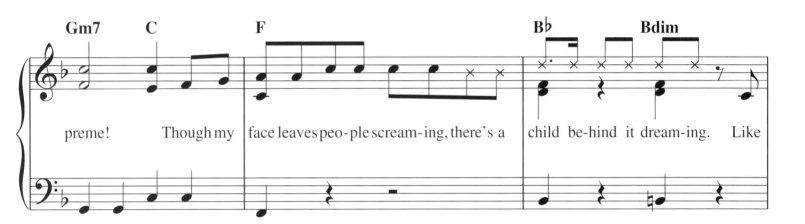

preme! Though my face leaves peo-ple scream-ing, there's a child be-hind it dream-ing. Like

ev-'ry-bod-y else, I've got a dream. *Thug Chorus:* Tor would like to quit and be a

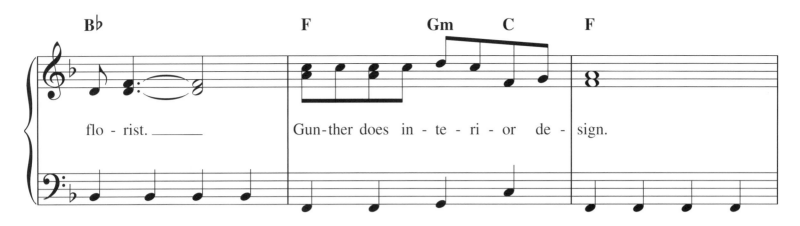

flo - rist. _____ Gun-ther does in - te - ri - or de - sign.

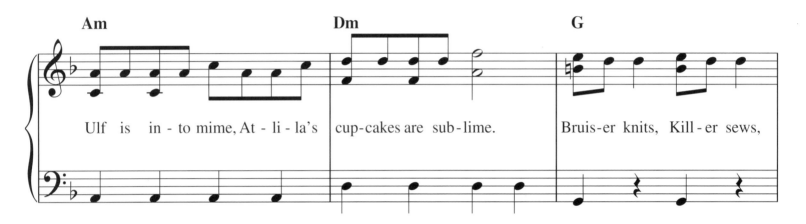

Ulf is in - to mime, At - li - la's cup-cakes are sub-lime. Bruis-er knits, Kill-er sews,

Fang does lit - tle pu - pet shows, and *Hook Hand Thug:* Vla - di - mir col-lects cer - am - ic *rit.* u - ni - corns.

Flynn: I have *a tempo* dreams like you, no, real- ly! Just much less touch-y feel- y. They

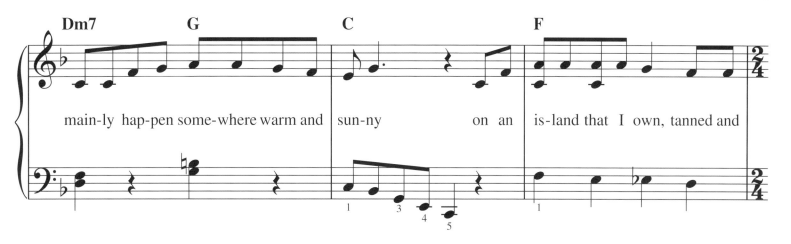

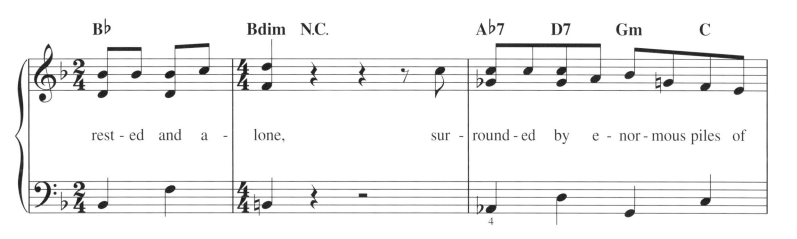

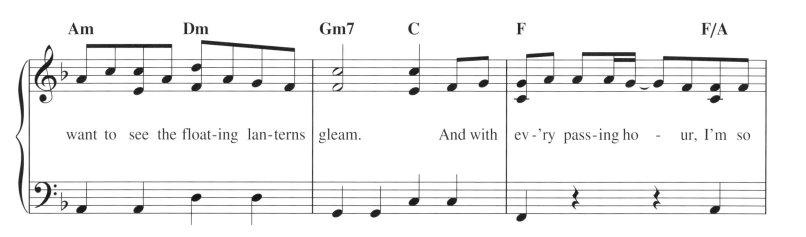

glad I left my tow- er. Like all you love- ly folks, I've got a dream. _____ She's got a

dream, _____ we've got a dream. So our dif-f'renc-es ain't real- ly that ex-

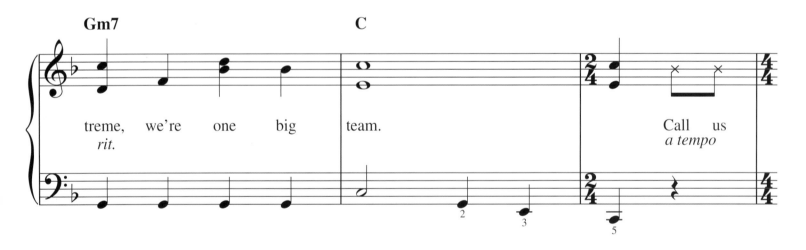

treme, we're one big team. Call us

Hook Hand Thug: Big Nose Thug: Thug Chorus:
bru - tal, sick, sa-dis- tic, and gro - tes- quely op - ti-mis-tic. 'Cause

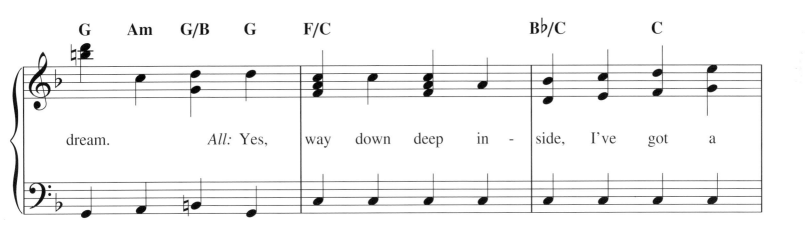

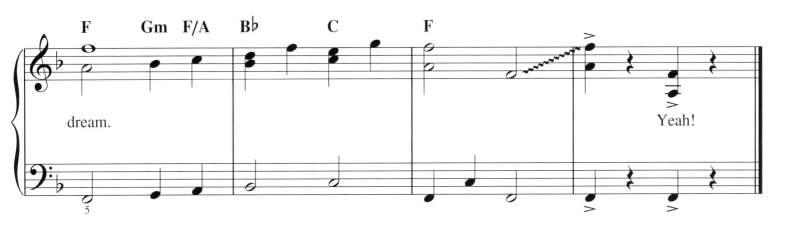

I SEE THE LIGHT

Music by ALAN MENKEN
Lyrics by DAVID SLATER

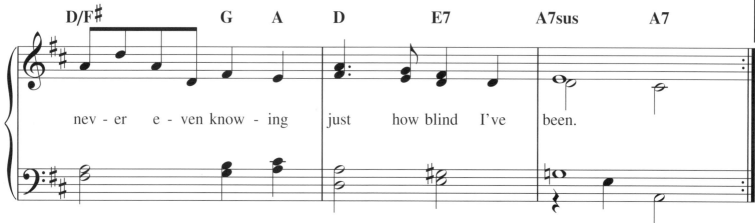

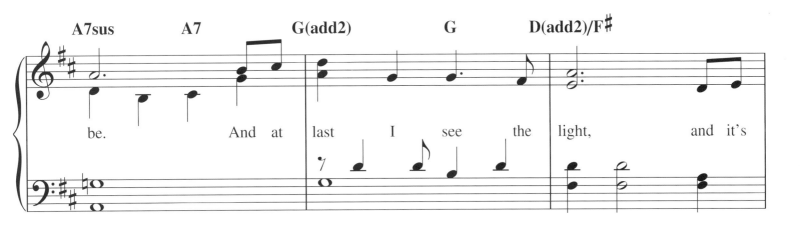

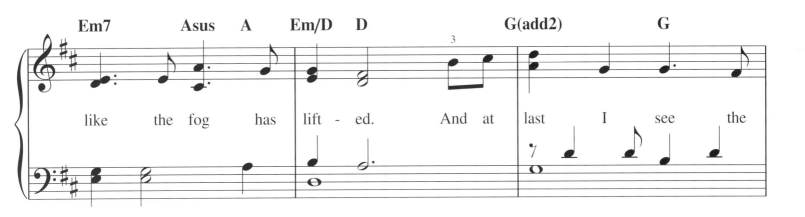

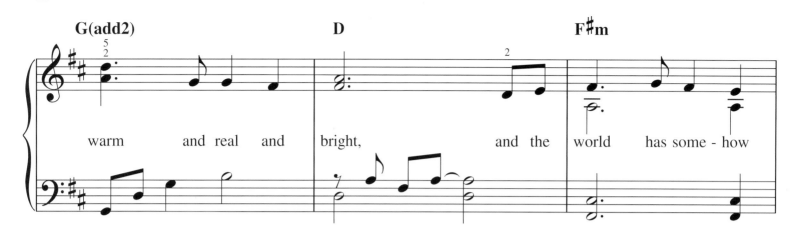

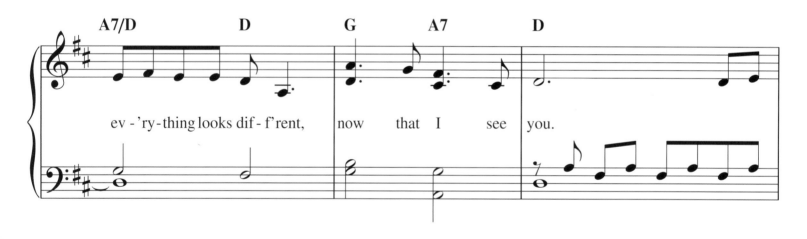

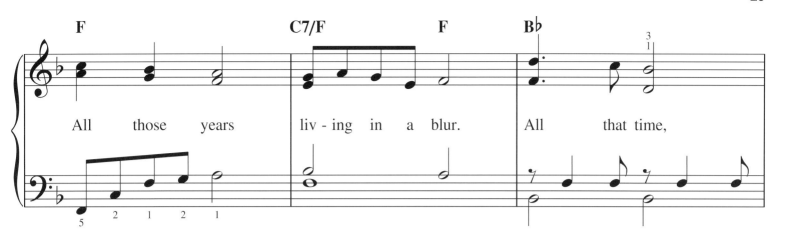

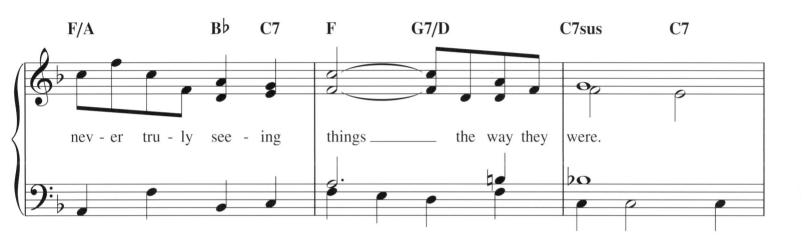

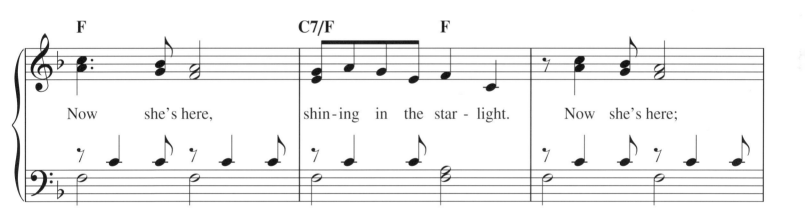

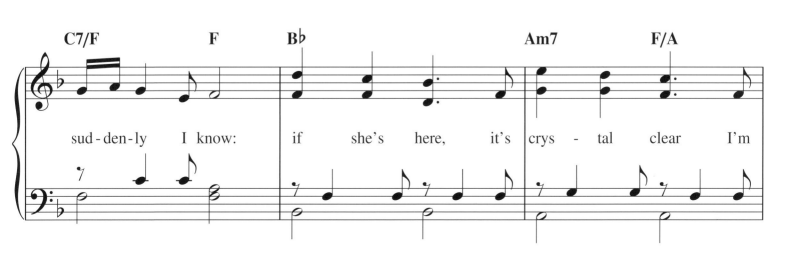

where I'm meant to go. *Both:* And at last I see the

light, *Flynn:* and it's like the fog has lift - ed. *Both:* And at

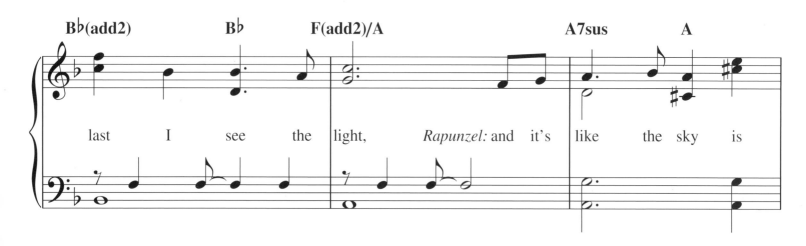

last I see the light, *Rapunzel:* and it's like the sky is

new. *Both:* And it's warm and real ___ and bright, ___ and the

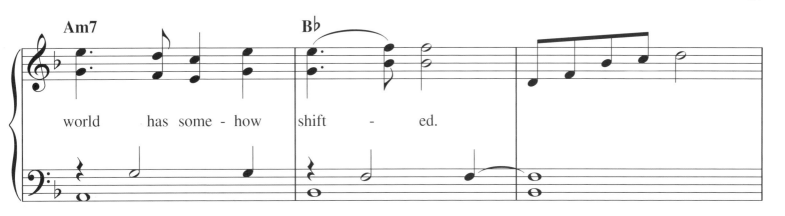

Am7 ... **B♭**

world   has   some - how   shift — ed.

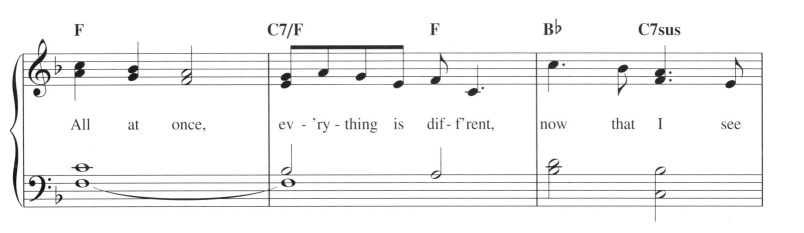

F   **C7/F**   **F**   **B♭**   **C7sus**

All   at   once,   ev - 'ry - thing   is   dif - f'rent,   now   that   I   see

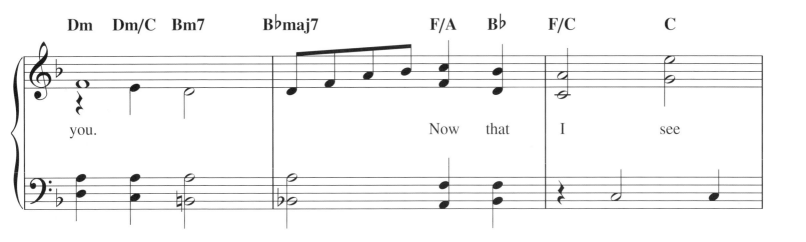

Dm   **Dm/C**   **Bm7**   **B♭maj7**   **F/A**   **B♭**   **F/C**   **C**

you.   Now   that   I   see

F

you.

HEALING INCANTATION

Music by ALAN MENKEN
Lyrics by GLENN SLATER

SOMETHING THAT I WANT

Music and Lyrics by
GRACE POTTER

She looked ___ out the win-dow, she walked ___
Right ___ when you think ___ you know ___

___ out the door, ___
___ what to say, ___

but she fol -
some-one comes _

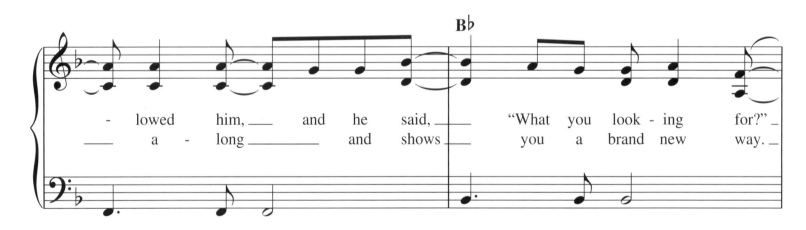

- lowed him, ___ and he said, ___ "What you look - ing for?" _
___ a - long ___ and shows ___ you a brand new way. _

She said: I
He said:

want some - thing that I want, _

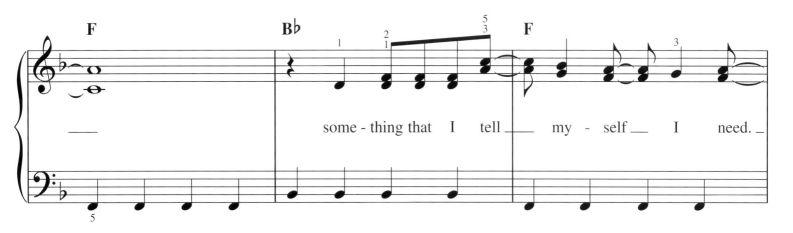

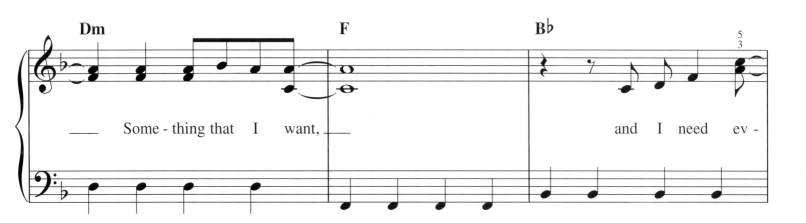

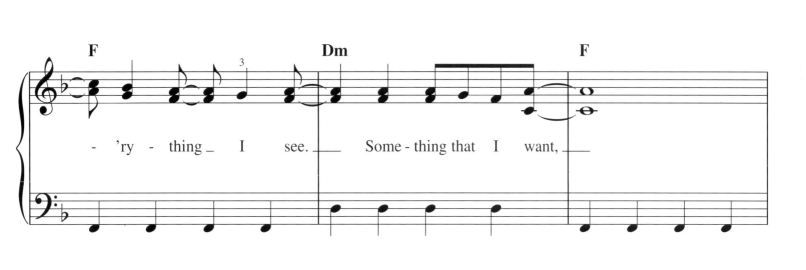

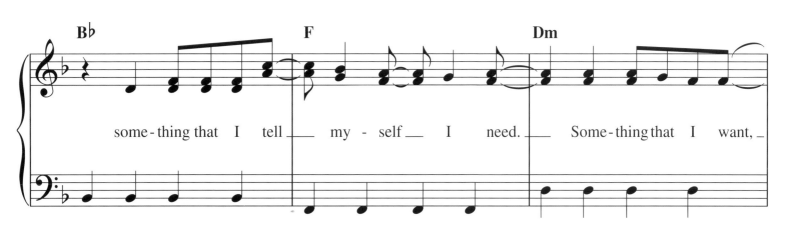

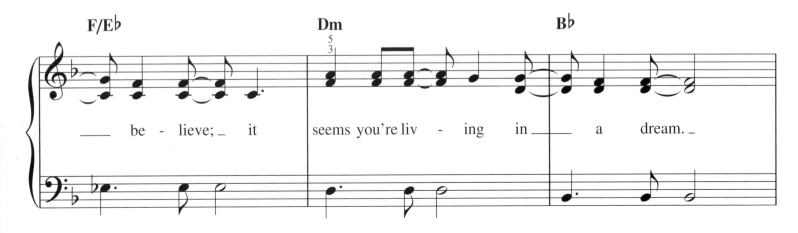

Don't you see — that what — you need — is stand - ing in front of you? —

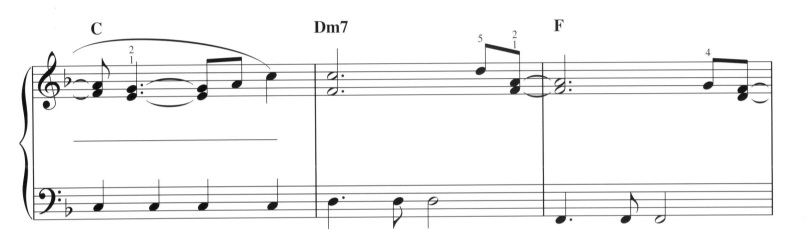

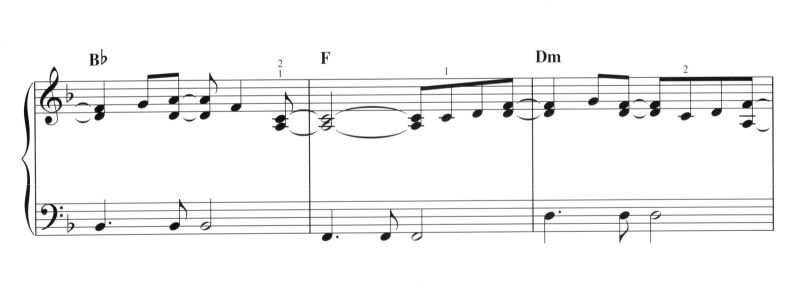

Oh, _____ I

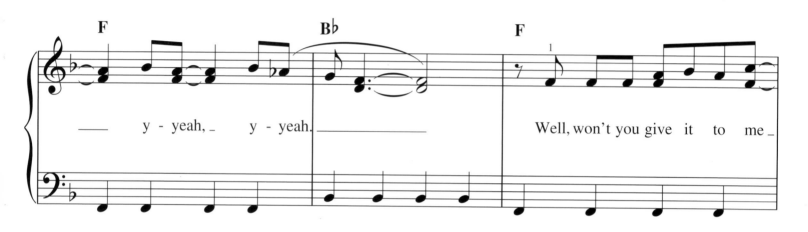

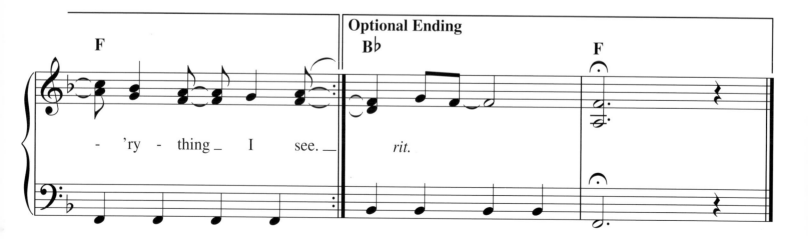